Text by Helen Slater
Illustrated by Alexander

This edition published in 1992 by
Joshua Morris Publishing, Inc.
221 Danbury Road, Wilton, CT 06897.

HOW TO BE A **STICKER BUILDER**

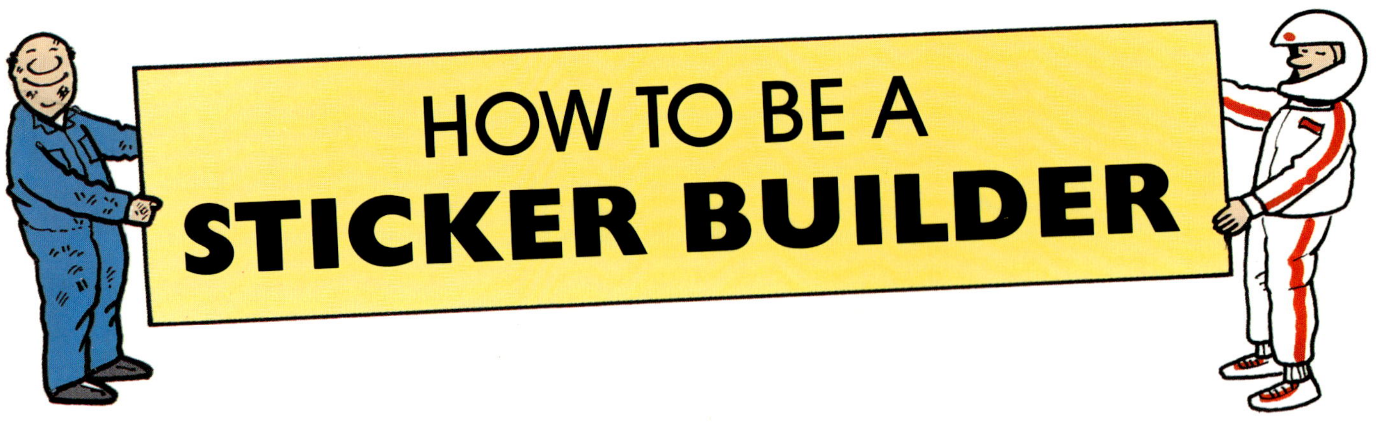

It's easy to be a sticker builder and build your own cars and trucks. Everything you need is on the sticker pages in the middle of this book.

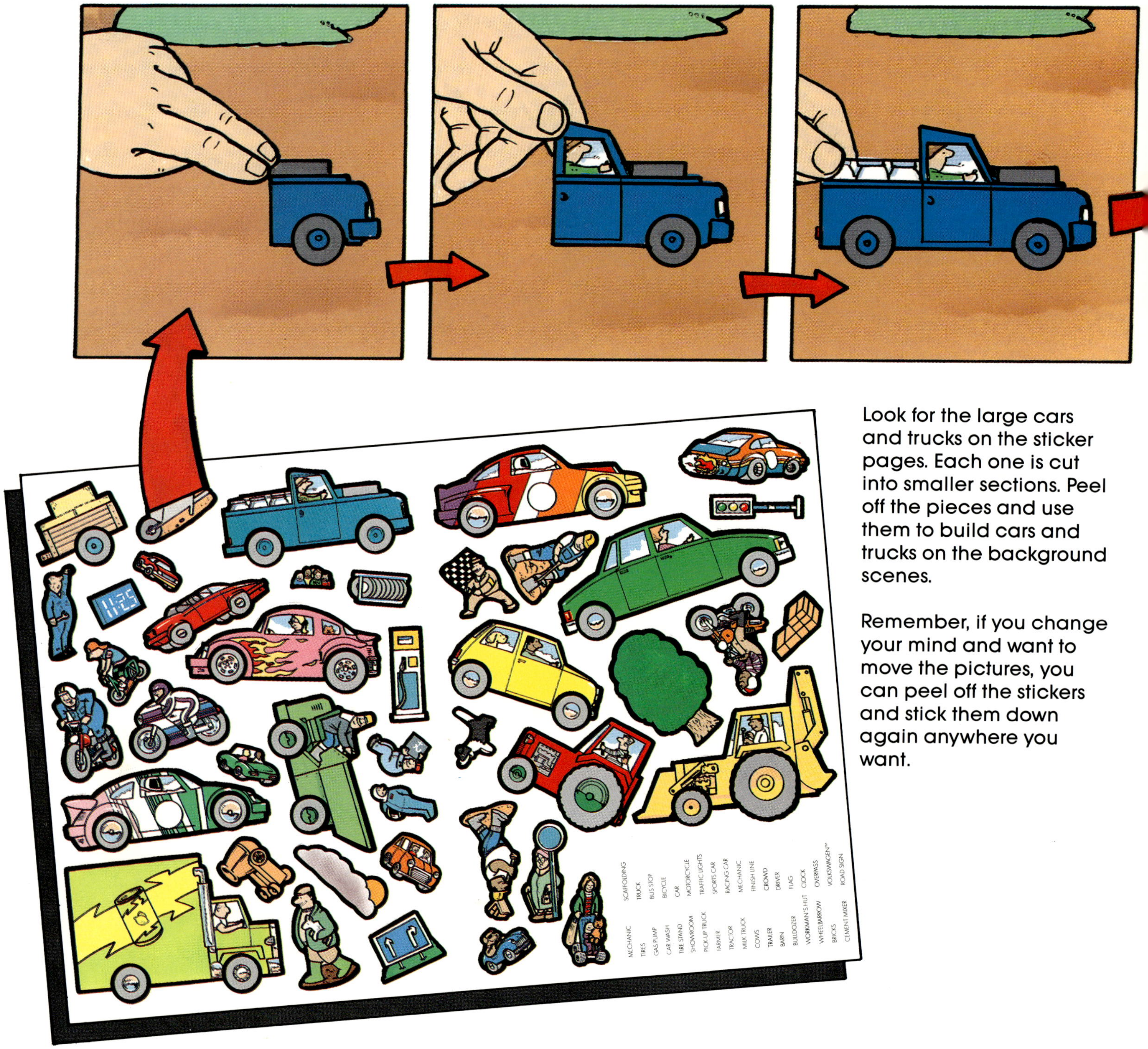

Look for the large cars and trucks on the sticker pages. Each one is cut into smaller sections. Peel off the pieces and use them to build cars and trucks on the background scenes.

Remember, if you change your mind and want to move the pictures, you can peel off the stickers and stick them down again anywhere you want.

Use some of the other stickers to fill up the rest of the scene. You can use any stickers that you think will look good on your picture.

If you can't decide which stickers to choose, the boxes at the bottom of each page will help you.

MIX AND MATCH

Don't forget that the sections from one of the large stickers will fit together with the sections from another.

That means that you can design your own crazy cars and trucks, like these!

ON THE FARM

Lots of people are coming and going in Farmer Giles' farmyard. The tractor is pulling a trailer full of hay and a truck has come to collect the milk. Can you build these vehicles using your stickers?
Another busy day!

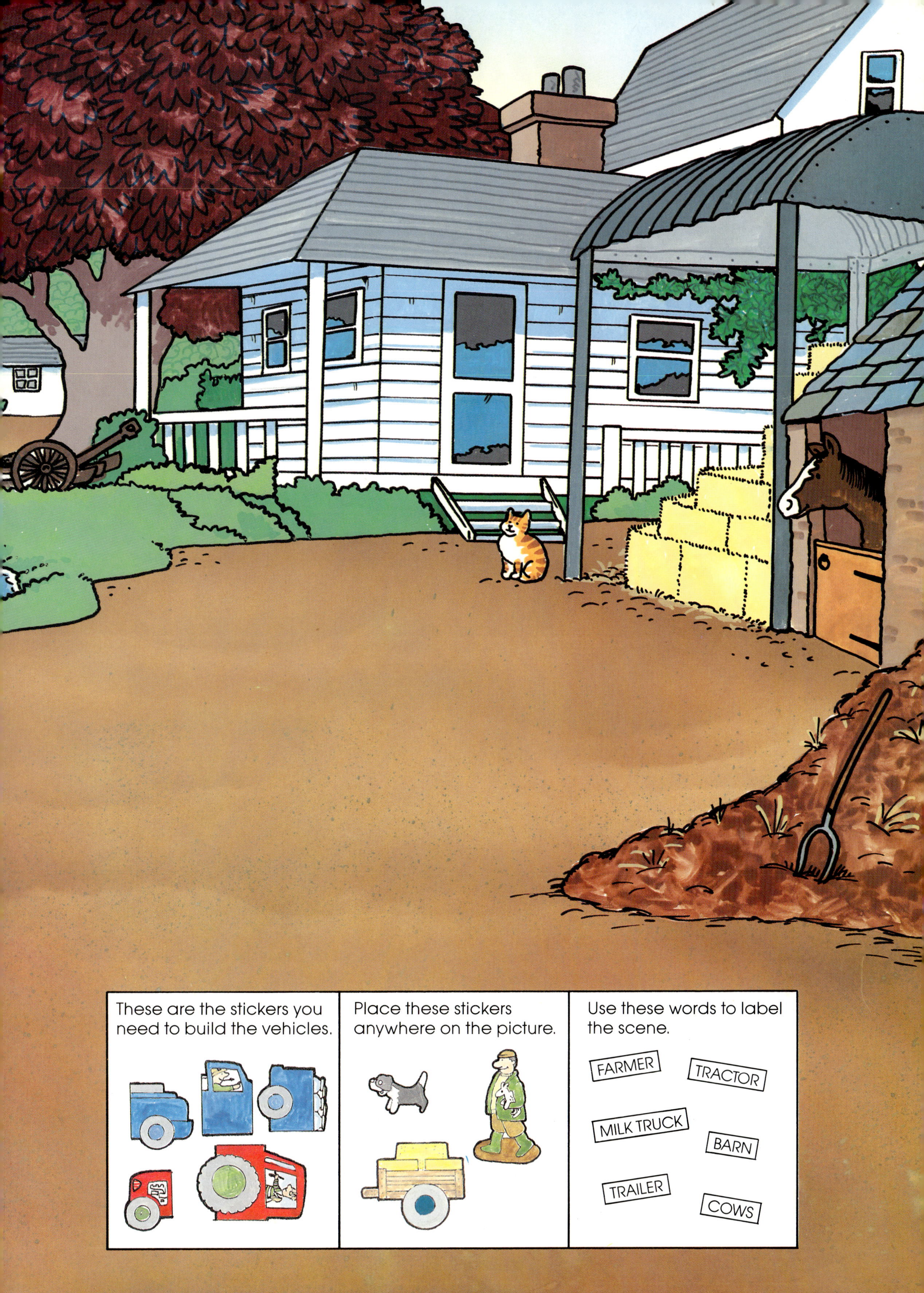

These are the stickers you
need to build the vehicles.
Place these stickers
anywhere on the picture.
Use these words to label
the scene.
FARMER
TRACTOR
MILK TRUCK
BARN
TRAILER
COWS

AT THE GARAGE

The garage is busy this afternoon. The mechanic is
mending one car, and other cars are waiting to be filled
with gas. What kind of cars are they? See how many
you can build with your stickers.
We're ready to go!

SPECIAL
These are the parts you need to build the cars.
Place these stickers anywhere on the picture.
Use these words to label the scene.
PICK-UP TRUCK
TIRE STAND
CAR WASH
MECHANIC
TIRES
SHOWROOM
GAS PUMP

IN THE TOWN

All the shops are busy today. Shoppers are arriving in their cars and a truck has come to deliver fresh food to the supermarket. Can you build the truck using your stickers?
Be careful when you cross the road!

These are the parts you need to build the truck.

Place these stickers anywhere on the picture.

Use these words to label the scene.

TRUCK
SPORTS CAR
BUS STOP
TRAFFIC LIGHTS
BICYCLE
MOTORCYCLE
CAR

THE BUILDING SITE

Everyone here is hard at work, digging holes, carrying
bricks and timber, and driving bulldozers and trucks.
Can you build a bulldozer using your stickers?
Time for a coffee break!

These are the parts you need to build the bulldozer.
Place these stickers anywhere on the picture.
Use these words to label the scene.
WHEELBARROW
BULLDOZER
WORKMAN'S HUT
CEMENT MIXER
BRICKS
SCAFFOLDING

AT THE RACE TRACK

The drivers are speeding around the track. The first past
the checkered flag will be the winner. What kind of
racing cars are they? See how many you can build
using your stickers.
Ready, set, go!

These are the parts you
need to build the cars.

Place these stickers
anywhere on the picture.

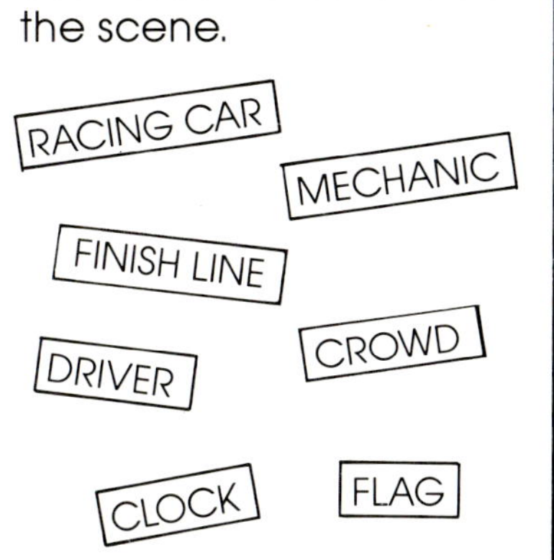
Use these words to label
the scene.
RACING CAR
MECHANIC
FINISH LINE
DRIVER
CROWD
CLOCK
FLAG

THE OPEN ROAD

Have you used all your picture and word stickers, or are there some still left over? Here's a scene for you to fill with any stickers you like. You can even borrow some from the other pictures.
Drive carefully!

Build up your knowledge of cars and trucks with these amazing fun facts!

Can you find the right stickers to match the shapes? You will find them on your completed pictures.

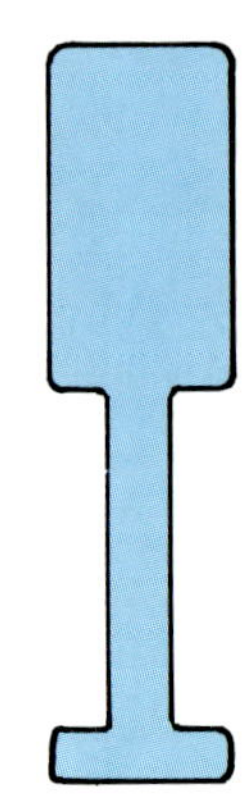

The first motorcycle ever made had a steam engine. The rider sat on top of the boiler!

The worst traffic jam in the world happened in France. The line of cars was nearly 180 kilometers (110 miles) long.

If all the cars and trucks in Hong Kong went onto the roads at the same time, there would be hardly any space between them!

Many people call this car "the Beetle" because its shape is just like a beetle!

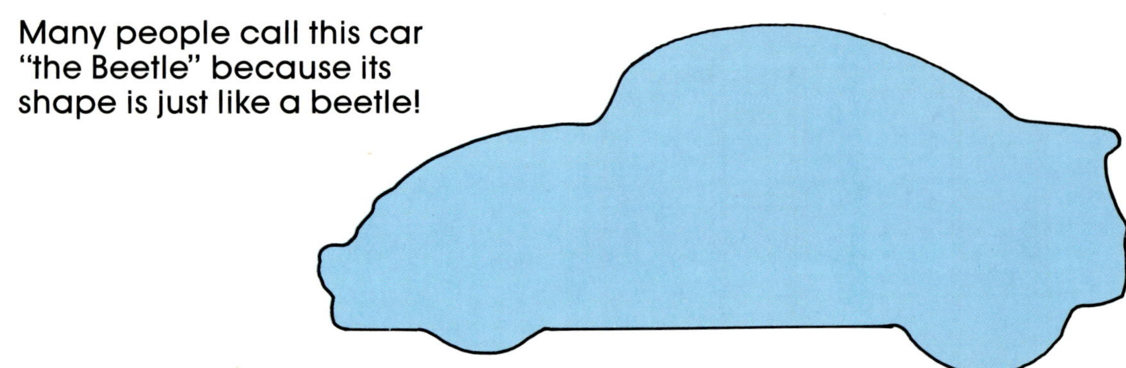